KIERA CLARKE

BOYS ARE SOOO ANNOYING

Cover Design and Chapter Illustrations by Aprilily

Imagination 2 Creation Publishing

Charleston, SC

Copyright © 2016 Holt Clarke

All rights reserved. No part of this book may be used or reproduced by any means, graphic, electronic, or mechanical, including photocopying, recording, taping or by any information storage retrieval system without the written permission of the publisher except in the case of brief quotations embodied in critical articles and reviews.

Books by Imagination 2 Creation Publishing may be ordered through booksellers or by contacting:

Imagination 2 Creation Publishing
www.HoltClarke.com

Because of the dynamic nature of the Internet, any web addresses or links contained in this book may have changed since publication and may no longer be valid. The views expressed in this work are solely those of the author and do not necessarily reflect the views of the publisher, and the publisher hereby disclaims any responsibility for them.

ISBN 978-0-9979335-0-5

To my annoying brother Luke,

because I love you.

INTRODUCTION

The book girls WANT every boy to read.

This book is to help boys learn what makes them sooo annoying, so they can stop being annoying.

KIERA CLARKE

REASON #1

Boys are weird.

Solution: Lose the weirdness.

REASON #2

Boys don't listen to you.

Solution: Listen when a girl is speaking.

REASON #3

Boys keep sneaking into your room.

Solution: Stay out unless invited in.

REASON #4

Boys throw temper tantrums.

Solution: Boys need to accept that no means no.

REASON #5

Boys want stuff that you have.

Solution: Learn to live with what you have.

REASON #6

Boys don't have manners.

Solution: Learn some, because it's a big deal to be well-mannered.

REASON #7

Boys are nosey.

Solution: Sometimes it's just none of their business.

REASON #8

Boys don't share games.

Solution: Share game time with others.

REASON #9

Boys always think they're silly.

Solution: Get a clue, you're not.

REASON #10

Boys barge in on your friends.

Solution: Go invite your friends over.

REASON #11

Boys are distracting.

Solution: Stop distracting and go talk to a tree.

REASON #12

Boys use potty talk words.

Solution: Go to the toilet if you want to use that language.

REASON #13

Boys talk a lot.

Solution: Learn to listen more.

REASON #14

Boys say bad words.

Solution: Only say nice words.

REASON #15

Boys are rude.

Solution: Be polite.

REASON #16

Boys mess with your food.

Solution: Mess with your own food.

REASON #17

Boys whine a lot.

Solution: Accept that you're not always going to get your way.

REASON #18

Boys interrupt constantly.

Solution: Stop talking when a girl is talking.

REASON #19

Boys do not share with you.

Solution: Sharing is caring.

REASON #20

Boys play with your toys.

Solution: Always ask first.

REASON #21

Boys are tattle-tales.

Solution: Nobody likes a tattle-tale.

REASON #22

Boys like to pull your hair.

Solution: Just cut it out. Not the hair, the pulling.

REASON #23

Boys ignore you.

Solution: Pay attention.

REASON #24

Boys always want to be first.

Solution: Share and take turns.

REASON #25

Boys steal your candy.

Solution: Don't mess with a girl's candy.

REASON #26

Boys blame girls for everything.

Solution: Just be honest.

REASON #27

Boys always get what they want.

Solution: This must change.

REASON #28

Boys hurt your feelings.

Solution: Say I'm sorry like you mean it.

REASON #29

Boys don't help enough.

Solution: Do your fair share.

REASON #30

Boys don't think anything is fair.

Solution: Excuses! Excuses! Stop making them.

REASON #31

Boys play rough.

Solution: Be gentle.

REASON #32

Boys are rude, crude dudes.

Solution: Be respectful and kind, not a behind.

REASON #33

Boys do not keep secrets.

Solution: Some things you just don't share.

REASON #34

Boys destroy your Minecraft world.

Solution: Don't mess with a girl's Minecraft world!

REASON #35

Boys don't pick up after themselves.

Solution: A girl likes a neat boy.

REASON #36

Boys are not always funny.

Solution: When a girl is not laughing, you're not funny.

REASON #37

Boys think they know it all.

Solution: Boys need girls, to be smarter. And it's TRUE.

REASON #38

Boys laugh inappropriately.

Solution: When girls are not laughing, it means it's serious. So stop laughing.

REASON #39

Boys don't clean up their dog's poop.

Solution: Sometimes you just gotta do it.

REASON #40

Boys don't like washing their hair.

Solution: If you want a girl to stare, then wash your hair.

REASON #41

Boys don't plan and rush.

Solution: Put more thought into it. Take your time, it'll be fine.

REASON #42

Boys ask a lot of questions.

Solution: Some questions you just don't ask.

REASON #43

Boys think they're so smart.

Solution: Girls usually have the right answer.

REASON #44

Boys don't follow directions.

Solution: Listen more and talk less.

REASON #45

Boys talk when they shouldn't.

Solution: Sometimes you just can't talk.

REASON #46

Boys get others in trouble.

Solution: Girls don't like getting in trouble when it's not their fault.

REASON #47

Boys will eat your dessert.

Solution: You can't eat other people's food.

REASON #48

Boys like to argue.

Solution: Sometimes you just got to save it for later.

REASON #49

Boys want to have first pick.

Solution: It's not all about you.

REASON #50

Boys annoy because they're boys.

Solution: Just accept that you need girls to be better boys.

LIFE LESSON FOR BOYS

Be more like girls and you'll be sooo less annoying.

Also by Kiera Clarke

Visit KieraClarke.com

Books By Holt Clarke

Visit HoltClarke.com

Visit HoltClarke.com

Visit HoltClarke.com

ABOUT THE AUTHOR

KIERA CLARKE is eight years old and is in the third grade. She enjoys playing Minecraft and Star Wars Battlefront. She lives in Charleston, South Carolina, with her family.

Visit KieraClarke.com for news and updates.

SPONSORED BY

SUPPORTING THE LITERARY ARTS

CharlestonianProperties.com

www.ingramcontent.com/pod-product-compliance
Lightning Source LLC
Chambersburg PA
CBHW070551300426
44113CB00011B/1874